The Mystery Trip

Written by Jenny Feely

Illustrated by Alex Stitt

Flying Start
to Literacy®

Daily News
WIN A MYSTERY TRIP FOR TWO!
JUST SOLVE THIS RIDDLE AND YOU COULD BE ON YOUR WAY.
In the sky you see my face,
As on I go from place to place.
One half of me is bright and light.
The other half is dark as night. What am I?
SEE PAGE TWO FOR DETAILS

Contents

Chapter 1: Just an ordinary day with the Grizzlegrots

Greta and Griffin Grizzlegrot could never agree on anything.

"The day is too cold," said Griffin Grizzlegrot.

"No, it's not," said Greta. "The air is lovely. It's fresh."

"Speaking of 'fresh', this fruit salad is not very fresh!" she said.

"Yes, it is!" said Griffin. "It is perfect. It's the best fruit salad I've ever eaten."

5

The Grizzlegrots could not stop arguing.
They argued all night and all day.

"The sun is too hot," said Greta.

"Too hot? Ridiculous!" said Griffin.
"The weather is perfect. I love sunshine.
I hate cold, dark nights."

"I don't," said Greta. "I love dark
nights because I can look at the moon.
I'd love to go to the moon."

"Me too!" said Griffin. "I would love
to go to the moon too."

The Grizzlegrots had finally agreed on
something!

Chapter 2: The mystery trip

One day Griffin saw a competition in the newspaper. The prize was a mystery trip for two people. To win the prize, you had to be the first one to solve a riddle and find out where the trip would take you. Griffin read out the riddle:

In the sky you see my face
As I go on from place to place.
One half of me is bright and light,
The other half is dark as night.
What am I?

Huh?

WIN A MYSTERY TRIP!

"Oh, I know," said Greta. "One half light, one half dark – a zebra."

"Don't be ridiculous," said Griffin. "When have you ever seen a zebra's face in the sky?"

"Well, you solve it then," said Greta.

"Let's think – the sun and the moon are bright and light," said Griffin.

"Yes, and the moon is dark as night on the side that we can't see," said Greta.

"It's the moon!" they both yelled. "The prize is a trip to the moon!"

As the Grizzlegrots were filling in the entry form for the competition, they noticed some extra information.

The form said: The winners of the competition must prove that they are fit enough to go on the mystery trip.

"Well, I'm fit enough to go to the moon," said Greta. "I'll be able to go."

"I'm fitter than you!" said Griffin.

AM AM AM AM AM!

"No, you're not," said Greta. "You puff
and pant when you are climbing up
the stairs.   You're not fit."

"Well you're not fit either," said Griffin.
"You can't even walk to the front gate
without taking a break."

"Let's call our doctor, Dr Bill, to come
and check how fit we are," said Greta.

Not! Not! Not!
Not! Not!

Chapter 3: Are they fit enough?

When Dr Bill arrived, the first thing he did was listen to Greta and Griffin's hearts.

"Your hearts are beating very fast," said Dr Bill. "When people are fit their hearts beat much more slowly."

Dr Bill checked their eyes and their ears and said, "Your sight and your hearing are fine."

Grrrr

Hmmm

Flub!
Flub!
Flub!
Flub!

DR BILL

Then he checked their bones and muscles.
"I want you to do 20 push-ups,"
said Dr Bill.

Greta and Griffin tried and tried but
they couldn't even do one push-up.
Dr Bill shook his head and said,
"Well, your bones are fine. But your
muscles are very weak and floppy."

DR
BILL

PuFF! PuFF! PuFF!

Next, Dr Bill asked Greta and Griffin to blow into a machine to measure how much oxygen could fit into their lungs.

"Oh, dear. Your lungs are not taking in as much oxygen as they should," said Dr Bill.

Then Dr Bill asked Greta and Griffin to run for five minutes without stopping. But after three minutes, they both collapsed in a heap on the floor.

"I have some very bad news,"
said Dr Bill.   "Neither of you is fit
enough to go to the moon."

"Oh, no!" cried the Grizzlegrots.

"Don't worry," said Dr Bill.   "I have a
fitness program that will help you to
get fit in time."

Chapter 4: The fitness program

"You need strong lungs to put oxygen in your blood," said Dr Bill. "You need a strong heart to pump the blood around your body. Your muscles need the oxygen in your blood to make them work."

"Exercise is what you need," said Dr Bill. "Every day you must walk or run. You must also do some push-ups and sit-ups."

"Walking is great, but running is not," said Griffin. "Running makes me puff and pant. Puffing and panting is awful."

"What is wrong with you?" said Greta. "Running is great. I love running."

"Stop arguing," said Dr Bill. "It doesn't matter whether you walk or run. Walking and running both make your lungs and heart strong. The important thing is to get moving."

"Well I can run further than you, Griffin," said Greta, as she ran off down the path.

"No, you can't!" said Griffin, as he ran after her.

Every day the Grizzlegrots argued about who could do the most push-ups or who was fastest or strongest.

And every day they got fitter and fitter.

Chapter 5: The waiting is over

As time went by, the Grizzlegrots became more and more impatient. At least 20 times a day they would check the letterbox hoping that they would get a letter about the competition.

Then one day a letter arrived.

"I'll open it," said Griffin.

"No, you won't," said Greta.

They pulled and tugged the letter back
and forth, back and forth until it ripped
in half and out fell . . . two tickets
to the moon.

"We've won, we've won! We're going
to the moon!" they both yelled, as they
danced around and around together.

Before Greta and Griffin could go to the moon they had to pass a fitness test with the doctor at the rocket base.

The doctor checked their hearts and lungs. "Hmm," he said.

He looked in their eyes and ears. "Quite good," he said. "But let's see how fit you are. You must run on this running machine for 30 minutes without stopping."

Go! Go!

Yes! Yes!

click!
Whirr!
RUMBLE!

Greta and Griffin began to run. Soon they had been running for five minutes. Then ten minutes. Then fifteen minutes.

Greta and Griffin puffed and panted, but they ran on and on and on.

At last the machine stopped. "Congratulations," said the doctor. "You have passed the test. You can go to the moon!"

Go! Go!

Yes! Yes!

RUMBLE!
RUMBLE!

Chapter 6: Off they go!

The next week the Grizzlegrots set off for the moon.

Of course they argued all the way there and all the way back.

But they did agree on one thing . . . going to the moon was wonderful!